Sara Swan Miller

Grasshoppers and Crickets of North America

Franklin Watts - A Division of Scholastic Inc.

New York • Toronto • London • Auckland • Sydney
Mexico City • New Delhi • Hong Kong
Danbury, Connecticut

Photographs © 2002: Animals Animals: 19 (Bill Beatty), 17 (Paul Berquist), 5 top left (Patti Murray); Bruce Coleman Inc.: 21 (Jeff Foott), 5 bottom right (Jan Taylor); Dwight R. Kuhn Photography: 1, 37, 42, 43; Photo Researchers, NY: 40 (Biophoto Associates), 25 (E.R. Degginger), 29 (Michael P. Gadomski), 7 top (Syd Greenberg), 6 (Hervy/Jacana), 7 bottom (K.M. Highfill), 14, 15 (David M. Schleser), 35 (David M. Schleser/Nature's Images, Inc.), 5 top right (John Serrao), cover (L. West/National Audubon Society); Robert & Linda Mitchell: 5 bottom left, 27, 39, 41; Thomas J. Walker: 31; Visuals Unlimited: 12, 13 (Bill Beatty), 33 (Wm. M. Johnson), 22, 23 (G and C Merker).

Illustrations by Pedro Julio Gonzalez and Steve Savage

The photo on the cover shows a spur throat grasshopper. The photo on the title page shows a jumping grasshopper.

Library of Congress Cataloging-in-Publication Data

Miller, Sara Swan.
Grasshoppers and crickets of North America / by Sara Swan Miller.
   p. cm. – (Animals in order)
   Summary: Explains the characteristics of different grasshoppers and crickets and how they are similar to or different than other members of the order, Orthoptera.
   ISBN 0-531-12170-4 (lib. bdg.)   0-531-16376-8 (pbk.)
   1. Grasshoppers—North America—Juvenile literature. 2. Crickets—North America—Juvenile literature. [1. Grasshoppers. 2. Crickets.] I. Title. II. Series.
QL508.A2 M55 2002
595.7'26—dc21   2001003563

Contents

Meet the Grasshoppers and Crickets

Have you ever walked through a field and stirred up grasshoppers hiding there? They leap away in all directions! Have you seen a cricket sitting on a rock, chirping away? Maybe you have watched a big, green katydid walking ever so slowly along a branch. "Katydid!" it calls.

Perhaps you thought these loud, long-legged insects might be related. You were right! Grasshoppers, crickets, and katydids all belong in the same group, or *order*, of insects called the *Orthoptera* (or-THOP-ter-uh). They have certain things in common that other insects don't share.

On the next page are four orthopterans. Can you tell why scientists put them all in the same order?

American grasshopper

True katydid

House cricket

Mole cricket

Traits of the Orthopterans

The first thing you probably noticed was these insects' very long legs. These legs have powerful muscles that make orthopterans incredible jumpers. If you had legs like theirs, you would be able to jump over a house!

Actually, this order is named for the insects' wings, not their legs. Orthoptera means "straight wings." The forewings of these insects are narrow, long, and leathery. When an orthopteran is resting, the forewings lie straight along its back and protect the hindwings underneath. The hindwings are broad and nearly transparent and fold up like a

Powerful leg muscles allow orthopterans to jump great distances.

fan. When one of these insects takes to the air, its forewings rise up and its hindwings fan out and make it fly.

All the orthopterans have large, flat-sided heads with *compound eyes* made up of hundreds of lenses. They also all have mouthparts that allow them to chew. These mouths are well suited to eating plants, although a few orthopterans also eat other insects, particularly dead ones. Because they eat plants, many orthopterans are thought of as pests, especially when they migrate in huge swarms.

When an orthopteran comes out of its egg, it looks like a small version of an adult, but without wings or sex organs. As the *nymph* grows, it sheds its skin several times. Each time, its wings are larger. These stages are known as *instars*. With the last instar, the nymph has fully grown wings and sex organs. This type of development is known as *incomplete metamorphosis* (met-uh-MOR-fuh-siss). Many other insects, such as bees, go through *complete metamorphosis*, from egg, to larva, to pupa, to adult.

Many male orthopterans make musical sounds. These sounds might be a warning, a way of defending territory, or a call to attract a mate. Some species make music by rubbing special veins on their wings together. Others rub pegs on their legs across a vein on their forewings.

The order Orthoptera includes pygmy grasshoppers, short-horned grasshoppers, long-horned grasshoppers and katydids, camel crickets, true crickets, and mole crickets. Sometimes grasshoppers are called "locusts," from their Latin name, *locusta*.

Orthopterans have compound eyes and chewing mouthparts.

A grasshopper crawls out of its old skin.

7

The Order of Living Things

A tiger has more in common with a house cat than with a daisy. A grasshopper is more like a butterfly than a jellyfish. Scientists arrange living things into groups based on how they look and how they act. A tiger and a house cat belong to the same group, but a daisy belongs to a different group.

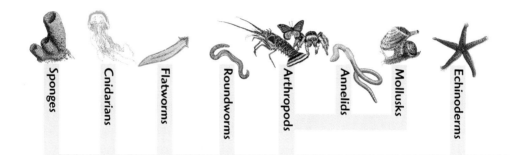

Sponges · Cnidarians · Flatworms · Roundworms · Arthropods · Annelids · Mollusks · Echinoderms

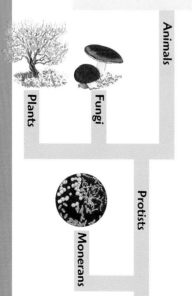

Animals · Plants · Fungi · Protists · Monerans

All living things can be placed in one of five groups called *kingdoms*: the plant kingdom, the animal kingdom, the fungus kingdom, the moneran kingdom, or the protist kingdom. You can probably name many of the creatures in the plant and animal kingdoms. The fungus kingdom includes mushrooms, yeasts, and molds. The moneran and protist kingdoms contain thousands of living things that are too small to see without a microscope.

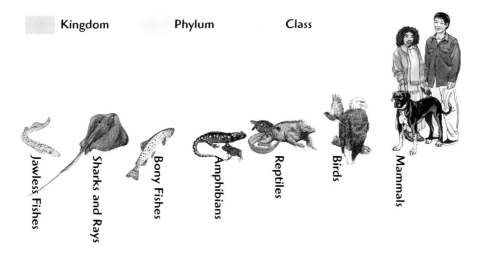

Kingdom Phylum Class

Jawless Fishes

Sharks and Rays

Bony Fishes

Amphibians

Reptiles

Birds

Mammals

Chordates

Because there are millions and millions of living things on Earth, some of the members of one kingdom may not seem all that similar. The animal kingdom includes creatures as different as tarantulas and trout, jellyfish and jaguars, salamanders and sparrows, elephants and earthworms.

To show that an elephant is more like a jaguar than an earthworm, scientists further separate the creatures in each kingdom into more specific groups. The animal kingdom can be divided into nine *phyla*. Humans belong to the chordate phylum. Almost all chordates have backbones.

Each phylum can be subdivided into many *classes*. Humans, mice, and elephants all belong to the mammal class. Each class can be further divided into orders; orders into *families*, families into *genera*, and genera into *species*. All the members of a species are very similar.

How Orthopterans Fit In

You can probably guess that orthopterans are part of the animal kingdom. They have more in common with spiders and snakes than they do with maple trees and morning glories.

Orthopterans belong to the arthropod phylum. All arthropods have a tough outer skin called an *exoskeleton*. Can you guess what other living things might be arthropods? Examples include spiders, scorpions, mites, ticks, millipedes, and centipedes. Some arthropods live in the ocean. Lobsters, crabs, and shrimps all belong to this group.

The arthropod phylum can be divided into a number of classes. Orthopterans belong to the insect class. Butterflies, ants, flies, and true bugs are also insects.

There are thirty different orders of insects. The orthopterans make up one of these orders. They have straight forewings, powerful back legs, and chewing mouthparts.

Scientists divide the orthoptera into ten or eleven families that contain hundreds of genera. These groups can be broken down into thousands of species. There are about 1,000 species of orthopterans in North America and more than 23,000 worldwide. Let's get to know some of these orthopterans!

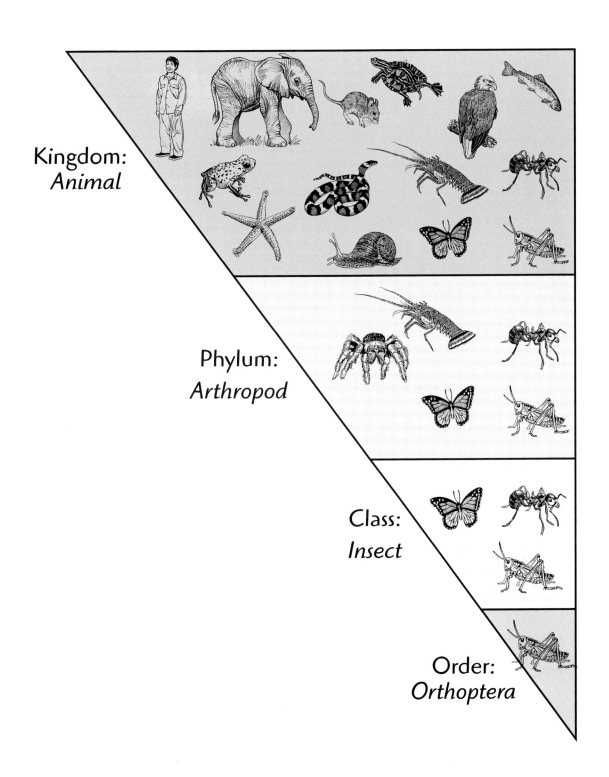

Kingdom: *Animal*

Phylum: *Arthropod*

Class: *Insect*

Order: *Orthoptera*

Pygmy Grasshoppers

FAMILY: Tetrigidae
COMMON EXAMPLE: Aztec pygmy grasshopper
GENUS AND SPECIES: *Paratettix aztecus*
SIZE: 1/4 to 1/2 inch (5 to 12 mm)

The Aztec pygmy grasshopper is very small—no bigger than the tip of your little finger. It is one of the smallest grasshoppers in the world.

But these teeny grasshoppers have big appetites! You might think that a grasshopper living in the desert would eat grasses, but not the Aztec pygmy grasshopper. It prefers algae and decaying plants. Many other grasshoppers can be quite destructive to crops, but farmers have no trouble with pygmy grasshoppers. By eating decaying plants, these insects help recycle them into fertile soil.

Aztec pygmy grasshoppers live on desert soil. They especially like the gravelly edges of the few small streams in the desert. In the damp soil they are more likely to find the algae they enjoy eating.

Being small has its advantages. Birds, mice, and other predators aren't likely to spot such tiny insects. They are also well camouflaged in grays

12

and browns that match the gravelly soil. As long as they hold still, they usually remain safe.

Most grasshoppers die when winter comes. Their eggs remain in the soil and hatch in the spring. But pygmy grasshoppers do it differently. The females live through the winter in the soil and come out to lay their eggs in the spring. It can be surprising to see a full-grown grasshopper so early in the spring, even such a small one.

Short-Horned Grasshoppers

FAMILY: Acrididae
COMMON EXAMPLE: Creosote bush grasshopper
GENUS AND SPECIES: *Bootettix argentatus*
SIZE: 3/4 to 1 inch (20 to 26 mm)

What is that odd, gritty, scratchy sound you can hear on summer nights in the desert? It's the mating call of the male creosote bush grasshoppers. They make their call by rubbing their sandpapery hindwings against veins in their forewings. The big hindwings act as loudspeakers, helping to make the call louder. That buzzing sound tells other males, "This is my territory! Go away!" At the same time, it calls to the females, "Where are you? Come here!"

How do the other grasshoppers hear the call? They don't have ears on their heads as we do. Instead, they have round, flat hearing organs called *tympana* (TIM-pan-uh) on the sides of their abdomens. See if you can find this grasshopper's tympana in the picture.

Can you guess how creosote bush grasshoppers got their name? They live and feed on the leaves

14

of creosote bushes, which grow in deserts in the Southwest. These bushes are named for their smell, which is like tar. We might not like the smell very much—certainly not enough to want to eat the leaves—but creosote bush grasshoppers like it just fine.

With its green body and brown speckles, this grasshopper is well camouflaged against the leaves of the creosote bush. It usually rests in the shade during the hot desert days. But if you get too close, it will flash its wings and quickly zoom away.

Short-Horned Grasshoppers

FAMILY: Acrididae

COMMON EXAMPLE: American grasshopper

GENUS AND SPECIES: *Schistocerca americana*

SIZE: 1 5/8 to 2 1/8 inches (40 to 55 mm)

In a sunny grove an American grasshopper clings to a grass stem, munching quietly on the leaves. With its brown and yellow coloring, it blends in well with the grass stems. Suddenly, a hungry egret comes stalking through the grass. But the grasshopper, ever alert, spots the egret easily. In an instant, the grasshopper spreads its wings and thrusts itself into the air with its big back legs. With a whistling buzz, it flies swiftly away to land high in a nearby orange tree. Soon it is munching away on the leaves.

American grasshoppers are such good fliers that they are also known as "bird grasshoppers." They are very common grasshoppers in the southeastern United States. Farmers are not at all fond of American grasshoppers because they do a lot of damage to crops. They feed on many different kinds of plants—corn, oats, cotton, tobacco, peanuts, citrus trees, and all kinds of garden vegetables. When they aren't feeding on crops, they eat Bermuda grass, dogwood or hickory leaves, and even crabgrass.

The adults usually roost in trees at night and fly down to feed on crops and plants on the ground during the day. The nymphs can't fly,

but they hop into fields and gardens, gobbling up crops as they go. In fact, the nymphs have even bigger appetites than the adults and do a lot more damage to plants.

The females lay two sets of eggs a year in the soil. Each cluster contains as many as 80 eggs. Imagine if all those grasshoppers survived! Luckily for the farmers, plenty of birds, mice, and even foxes love crunching up tasty grasshoppers.

Short-Horned Grasshoppers

FAMILY: Acrididae

COMMON EXAMPLE: Migratory grasshopper

GENUS AND SPECIES: *Melanopus sanguinipes*

SIZE: 1 to 1 3/8 inches (25 to 34 mm)

It's not hard to guess how the migratory grasshoppers got their name. From time to time they take off in great swarms and migrate together to new and better feeding grounds. The swarming grasshoppers may fly 30 miles (48 km) a day for several days until they all settle down in a field. In 1938 a swarm of migratory grasshoppers traveled 575 miles (925 km) all the way from South Dakota to Saskatchewan.

Usually the grasshopper swarms fly no more than 25 feet (7.5 m) above the ground. But airplane pilots have met them flying nearly 2 miles (3 km) up in the air! When they finally reach their destination, there may be as many as 140 grasshoppers per square yard. Then they all set to work eating everything in sight.

As you might guess, farmers don't like migratory grasshoppers. They have huge appetites and cause more crop damage than any other species of grasshopper in North America. A swarm of them can destroy a whole field of corn, wheat, or barley. They also feed on bushes, trees, and vegetables.

Usually, there are not enough migratory grasshoppers in a single area to do much damage. During cool, wet springs with heavy rains,

most of the young nymphs die. But if the spring and fall are warm, the grasshopper population gets bigger and bigger. Finally, the grasshoppers run out of food and fly off to greener pastures.

Long-Horned Grasshoppers

FAMILY: Tettigoniidae
COMMON EXAMPLE: Mormon cricket
GENUS AND SPECIES: *Anabrus simplex*
SIZE: 1 to 2 3/8 inches (25 to 60 mm)

You probably could never guess how Mormon crickets got their name. They are named after the Mormons, a religious group that moved into Utah around 1848. No sooner had the Mormon pioneers planted their crops than thousands of crickets showed up. They began devouring everything the pioneers had planted. Suddenly, flocks of gulls arrived and gobbled up the crickets. The crops were saved!

Many other birds and several mammals love eating Mormon crickets, too, including crows, hawks, coyotes, and rodents. There is even a type of digger wasp that eats these crickets. All of these predators help keep the numbers of Mormon crickets under control.

The Native Americans also used to enjoy eating these insects. Archeologists discovered a cave in Wyoming where they found the cooked remains of hundreds of Mormon crickets in a roasting pit.

Mormon crickets have small, useless wings, but they still migrate long distances. When there are too many of them in one area, both the nymphs and the adults crawl and hop in groups to fresh pastures. The adults can travel up to a mile (1.6 km) a day. In a single season they may travel as many as 50 miles (80 km).

In the spring, the males call to the females by rubbing their raspy front wings together. After mating, a female lays her eggs one by one in the soil with her very long *ovipositor*, or egg layer. She may lay as many as a hundred eggs! But so many animals like eating the young that most of them don't live to adulthood. It's a good thing for farmers that these hungry crickets have so many predators!

Camel Crickets and Their Kin

FAMILY: Gryllacrididae
COMMON EXAMPLE: Jerusalem cricket
GENUS AND SPECIES: *Stenopelmatus fuscus*
SIZE: 1 1/8 to 2 inches (30 to 50 mm)

The large, big-headed Jerusalem crickets are very common in the West, but you won't see them hopping about in the open during the day-time. If you turn over a rock or a board, though, you might find one hiding out in the dark. It uses its thick, armored front legs to dig down into the soil.

At first sight, a Jerusalem cricket looks scary. It has a large, human-like head with big jaws, and its back legs have sharp spines. But these fright-ening-looking crickets are harmless unless you pick one up. Then it might give you a little nip.

Jerusalem crickets have no wings, but they don't need to fly. They crawl about on the ground or dig into the sandy soil to find their food. They nibble on roots and tubers and some-times eat bits of dead animals. Some people call them potato bugs because they will sometimes

22

munch on potatoes. However, farmers don't think of them as serious pests because they don't do much damage to crops.

Jerusalem crickets move much more slowly than other crickets do. At mating time in the spring they are even slower. The male calls to the female by rubbing a hind leg against its abdomen. But mating is dangerous for a male Jerusalem cricket. After mating, the female eats him! That may sound horrible to you, but the female needs the extra protein to grow her eggs.

Mole Crickets

FAMILY: Gryllotalpidae
COMMON EXAMPLE: Northern mole cricket
GENUS AND SPECIES: *Neocurtilla hexadactyla*
SIZE: 3/4 to 1 3/8 inches (20 to 35 mm)

You would probably never guess that northern mole crickets are very common in the East because you hardly ever see them. They spend most of their time burrowing underground, digging with their shovel-like front legs. Below the ground, they feed on the roots of grasses and other plants.

Mole crickets are well suited to a life underground. They are great diggers and are covered with a thick coat of fine hair that keeps soil from sticking to their bodies. On their front legs they have shears, which they use to snip off roots. Even though they live underground, they do have wings and can fly quite well when they need to.

Like many other orthopterans, mole crickets can be pests. They may damage crops and garden plants when they feed on their roots. They can do a lot of damage to golf courses too. We humans may not like them much, but many other animals do. Birds and moles find them very tasty.

At mating time a male calls to the females with an odd growling sound, which is made louder by the shape of his burrow. The burrow in which he lives opens on the surface of the ground with two cone-shaped funnels, which act as loudspeakers.

The females lay their eggs in clusters among the plant roots, which the nymphs can feed on when they hatch. Unlike most insects, female mole crickets guard their eggs and nymphs. Their nipping shears make good weapons!

Lubber Grasshoppers

FAMILY: Acrididae

COMMON EXAMPLE: Eastern lubber grasshopper

GENUS AND SPECIES: *Romalea guttata*

SIZE: 2 1/2 to 3 1/8 inches (60 to 80 mm)

Did you know that "lubber" is the name for a big, clumsy person? The lubber grasshopper is certainly well named! It's large and thick-bodied and amazingly clumsy. Lubbers have small wings and cannot fly. They can jump only short distances. Mainly, they get around by crawling slowly and awkwardly over the ground.

At times, lubbers migrate together in large swarms, creeping through fields and across roads. Sometimes there are so many crossing a road that their squished bodies make the road slippery enough to cause accidents.

Even though these grasshoppers are slow and clumsy, they have good ways of defending themselves from enemies. Their bright yellow, red, and black coloring sends a strong message to other creatures: Don't eat me! I taste awful! The poisons in their bodies are powerful enough to kill the birds that make the mistake of eating them. Even larger animals, such as opossums, can get violently sick after eating a lubber grasshopper.

If their bright colors don't scare off enemies, lubbers have another trick they can use for defense. They secrete a foamy spray from their

thorax (the second segment of their bodies) that can be very irritating. As the foam squirts out, it makes a loud, hissing sound. That's enough to scare off anyone!

Like many grasshoppers, lubbers mate and lay their eggs in the summer. Each female digs a hole in the soil with the tip of her abdomen. She lays up to fifty eggs and covers them with a foamy froth. The eggs stay warm underground all winter, until they hatch in the spring.

Katydids

FAMILY: Tettigoniidae
COMMON EXAMPLE: True katydid
GENUS AND SPECIES: *Pterophylla camellifolia*
SIZE: 1 3/4 to 2 1/8 inches (45 to 55 mm)

If you live in the eastern half of the United States, you can hear true katydids calling all through the summer nights. "Katy DID!" "Katy DIDN'T!" "Katy DID!" "Katy DID!" "Katy DIDN'T!" It sounds like a crowd of people having a huge argument...did she or didn't she?

Of course, the katydids aren't really arguing. They're calling to find mates. For most orthopterans, it's the males that do the calling. But female katydids call just as loudly as the males do.

Katydids have roughened patches on the overlapping bases of their front wings. When they rub their wings together, they vibrate. Katydids can be really loud!

Can you find a katydid's ears? They're not on its head as our ears are. They're not even on its body as a grasshopper's are. A katydid's tympana are on the base of its front legs.

Katydids are in the family of long-horned grasshoppers. None of these grasshoppers actually have horns. Their so-called "horns" are really their antennae. These sensitive antennae help them find their way around.

Katydids live in leafy trees and shrubs and are well camouflaged. Their humped, green bodies make them look like leaves. If you do

spot one and try to pick it up, it will defend itself by spitting up some brown saliva. You wouldn't want a handful of that!

Tree Crickets

FAMILY: Grillidae
COMMON EXAMPLE: California tree cricket
GENUS AND SPECIES: *Oecanthus californicus*
SIZE: 1/2 to 5/8 inch (13 to 15 mm)

You might guess that the place to look and listen for California tree crickets is in California. It's true that they are very common there, but they also live in Nevada, Texas, Oklahoma, Utah, and Idaho. If you live in any of those states, you have probably heard these tree crickets trilling in the trees on summer nights.

Only the males trill their mating songs. Like katydids, they make their calls by rubbing rough spots at the base of their wings together. Their mates, like katydids, hear the calls with tympana on the base of their front legs.

Tree crickets have an odd way of mating. When a female finds a male, she nudges him until he stops trilling. Then she nibbles a secretion that comes from a gland on his back. This liquid helps get her ready for mating and laying eggs.

Like other crickets, a California tree cricket has a long ovipositor. She uses it to cut rows of tiny holes into tree bark. Before she lays her eggs in a hole, she dabs a little bit of her droppings inside. The droppings make a glue that holds each egg in place.

The eggs are protected inside the hole all through the winter. In the spring the eggs hatch and the tiny nymphs emerge. They set to

work nibbling on flowers, leaves, and fruit. The small nymphs grow very slowly. Finally, by midsummer they have grown into adults. Then they start gobbling up aphids and caterpillars and getting ready for mating time.

Tree Crickets

FAMILY: *Grillidae*
COMMON EXAMPLE: Snowy tree cricket
GENUS AND SPECIES: *Oecanthus fultoni*
SIZE: 1/2 to 5/8 inch (13 to 15 mm)

You can listen for snowy tree crickets almost anywhere in North America except in the southeastern states. On summer nights, the males hang onto leaves or twigs and call to the females with a pretty, trilling song.

Did you know that you can figure out what the temperature is by listening to snowy tree crickets calling? It's true. Like other insects, these tree crickets are cold-blooded. When it is warmer, their metabolisms speed up. When it is colder, their metabolisms slow down. So the warmer it is, the faster they chirp.

You can figure out the exact temperature outside using a watch and some simple arithmetic. To find out the temperature in Fahrenheit, count the number of chirps you hear in 13 seconds and then add 40. So if you hear 20 chirps, you know it's 60 degrees outside. If you want to know the temperature in Celsius, count the number of chirps you hear in 7 seconds and then add 5. With snowy tree crickets around, who needs a thermometer?

This formula works only for snowy tree crickets, however, so you want to make sure you are listening to the right species. California tree crickets look and sound a lot like snowy tree crickets. Both are

pale green and the males have paddle-shaped wings. But California tree crickets have reddish dots on their antenna, while snowy tree crickets have black spots. You'll need sharp eyes and a magnifying glass to see the difference.

Crickets

FAMILY: Gryllidae
COMMON EXAMPLE: House cricket
GENUS AND SPECIES: *Acheta domesticus*
SIZE: 5/8 to 3/4 inch (15 to 19 mm)

Back in the days when people heated their homes with fireplaces, a house cricket was known as the "cricket on the hearth." The crickets liked to sit near the warm fire on cold nights. People used to enjoy their sweet trilling calls—chiiirp, chiiirp, chiiirp! Many people thought that having a house cricket in their homes was a sign of good luck.

Now that most people have central heating, house crickets might be living anywhere in the house. They hide during the day and come out at night to forage for food. They love crumbs and vegetable scraps. They may even get into a garbage can to enjoy carrot peels and other vegetable refuse. House crickets also live in bakeries and breweries, where they can nibble on grains and crumbs.

Unlike crickets that live outdoors, house crickets mate and lay eggs all year round. You can find both nymphs and adults in any season. The males' mating calls are long, continuous trills. Some people say that it's hard to sleep when a male is calling in the bedroom!

Females use their long ovipositors to lay their eggs in dark crevices and cracks. Each female has her own territory and releases a chemical that keeps other females away. The others have to find

their own spots in which to start their families. That way, all the nymphs will find plenty of food without competing with each other.

Camel Crickets

FAMILY: Gryllacrididae
COMMON EXAMPLE: Spotted camel cricket
GENUS AND SPECIES: *Ceuthophilus maculatus*
SIZE: 3/8 to 3/4 inch (10 to 19 mm)

If you have a damp basement, chances are that you have camel crickets too. But you can't tell by listening for them because they are completely silent. They have no sound-making organs and no hearing organs, either.

But if you go down to the basement, you may spy a couple of camel crickets hiding in dark, secluded areas. Look carefully in damp corners or behind some old, moldy boxes. These crickets have humped backs like a camel. Their glossy brown bodies are streaked with yellowish- or reddish-brown. All of them have very long antennae and huge back legs, but no wings.

Since they can't see in the dark and can't hear, camel crickets use their long antennae, excellent sense of smell, and the sensitive bristles on their legs to find their way about and to search for food and mates. Their sensitive antennae also alert them to hungry spiders, centipedes, and mice lurking in ambush for a tasty meal. In the damp, dark places where camel crickets live, they feed on fungi, molds, and decaying plant matter. They sometimes eat dead insects, even their own relatives.

Spotted camel crickets are also known as "cave crickets" because

they live in damp caves. They also hide under logs or stones, under tree bark, or even in the soil—wherever it is dark and damp.

The females use their long ovipositors to lay their eggs one by one into the soil. The ones that live in caves often lay their eggs in bat droppings. It may be smelly, but it makes a warm nest!

Crickets

FAMILY: Gryllidae
COMMON EXAMPLE: Field cricket
GENUS AND SPECIES: *Gryllus pennsylvanicus*
SIZE: 5/8 to 1 inch (15 to 25 mm)

If this cricket is called a "field" cricket, what is it doing in your house? For the most part field crickets do live outside in the fields, but when the fall air turns cold, they may find their way into houses. Lured by the warmth, they sneak in through cracks and holes.

Field crickets look a lot like house crickets. How can you tell the difference? House crickets are yellowish-brown and their hind wings stick out beyond their abdomens. Field crickets are dark reddish-brown and their wings are a little shorter than their abdomens.

Outdoors, field crickets feed on seeds and seedlings and on small fruits. They sometimes also eat dead or dying insects. Indoors, they can find all kinds of treats, including bread crumbs and other bits of plant food that have fallen to the floor.

Most people don't mind sharing a crumb with a field cricket, but the crickets don't stop there. They also like chewing on wool and fur. Usually, people blame the holes in their sweaters on clothes moths when field crickets may be the real culprits. The best way to keep field crickets away from your clothing is to plug any holes and cracks in your house that they can sneak through.

Field crickets lay their eggs deep in the soil in the late summer.

Then, unless they can find a warm house to live in, the adults die. The eggs, safe underground, hatch in the spring. It takes three months and ten instars before the nymphs finally grow into adults.

Enjoying Crickets, Grasshoppers, and Katydids Outdoors

How would you like to get to know some orthopterans better? Late spring, summer, and early fall are the best times to look and listen for them in fields and gardens. Before you go off to find them, you need a plastic hand lens, a field guide to insects, and a journal to record what you see and hear.

You can sometimes find grasshoppers perched on blades of grass.

Listen for the sounds of male grasshoppers and crickets calling for their mates. Can you find who is making the sound? Look carefully on grass stems or under stones. When you find an orthopteran, move very slowly. A scared grasshopper or cricket will leap away quickly.

With your hand lens, try to get a close-up look. Can you find its mouth and ears? How is it making its call? Is it eating anything? What color is it? Try to get a good look at its long, strong back legs.

Draw a picture of what you see in your journal. Then describe how the orthopteran you found moves, what it's doing, where and when you found it, and anything else you notice. You can use your field guide to find out what kind of cricket or grasshopper you found.

Females are harder to find than males because they are silent. If you do find a female hiding in the grass or under a rock, you can recognize her by her long ovipositor. Males, of course, don't have ovipositors.

An early evening during the summer is a good time to listen for katydids call-ing from the trees. In your journal, write

Try to examine an orthopteran's head and features up close.

down what kind of sounds they make. The true katydids call out "Katy DID!" "Katy DIDN'T!" Try counting how many times you hear "Katy DID!" and how many times you hear "Katy DIDN'T." Which call do they make the most? Did Katy do it or not? Write down what you find out.

You may want to search among the tree leaves with a flashlight. Katydids are well camouflaged, but you may be able to spot one if you look carefully. If you do find one, watch it for a while. Can you see how it makes its song? How does it move? Draw a picture of the katydid and write down what you learned.

41

Cricket Guests

Crickets can be fun guests. Many people keep them as pets because they sing such sweet songs. Some people in China have special cricket cages so they can carry their little music-makers with them wherever they go.

Set up a guest home for your orthopteran to live in while you observe it.

Before you bring any crickets home, though, you need to make a guest house for them. An aquarium with a screen top works best. Put a layer of gravel on the bottom and a layer of soil on top of the gravel. Plant some grasses and little plants in the soil to make your guests feel at home. Add some rocks for them to climb on and hide under. Spray the soil with water so the plants will grow.

You can feed the crickets grasses and weeds, or you can give them bread and pieces of lettuce. They need water to drink too. Wet a sponge with water and put it in a small dish. Your guests can suck water from the sponge, but they won't fall into the water and drown.

To find crickets, take some small plastic jars with lids into a field and turn over stones. Be ready to move quickly before the crickets

Crickets and grasshoppers can be transported in jars.

leap away. If you're lucky, you can collect both males and females to take home.

Once your guests feel comfortable in their new homes, they are fun to listen to and watch. You can see how they eat and what foods they like best. You can listen to their sweet songs and figure out how they make them.

How about keeping a guest book? You can draw pictures of your guests and write down things you discover about them. How much do they eat? How big are they? Where are their ears?

You might want to use a clock with a second hand to find out how often a male chirps. Then you might try putting one in a jar in the refrigerator for just a few minutes. How many times does it chirp when it's chilly? Does it speed up again when you put it back in its guest house?

As long as you give them food and keep their sponge wet, you can enjoy your cricket guests for many days. You could become a real cricket expert! After a week or so, though, you should take them back to where you found them and let them go free.

Words to Know

class—a group of creatures within a phylum that shares certain characteristics

complete metamorphosis—the term for the development of insects that go through an egg stage, a larval stage, and a pupal stage before becoming adults

compound eye—the type of eye most insects possess, which is made up of many lenses

exoskeleton—a hard outer skin that all arthropods possess

family—a group of creatures within an order that shares certain characteristics

genus (plural **genera**)—a group of creatures within a family that shares certain characteristics

incomplete metamorphosis—the term for the development of insects that go through an egg stage and a nymphal stage before becoming adults

instar—a stage in the development of an immature insect as it grows to adulthood

locusta—the Latin name for grasshoppers. Some grasshoppers are called "locusts."

nymph—the name for the young of insects that undergo incomplete metamorphosis

order—a group of creatures within a class that shares certain characteristics

orthoptera—the name for the order that includes grasshoppers, katydids, and crickets

ovipositor—the egg-laying organ of an insect

phylum—a group of creatures within a kingdom that shares certain characteristics

species—a group of creatures within a genus that shares certain characteristics. Members of the same species can mate and produce young.

thorax—the segment of an insect's body from which its legs grow

tympanum (plural **tympana**)—the hearing organ of an insect

Learning More

Books

Johnson, Sylvia A. *Chirping Insects*. Minnetonka: Lerner, 1986.

Leahy, Christopher. *Peterson's First Guide to Insects*. Boston: Houghton Mifflin, 1987.

Pascoe, Elaine. *Crickets and Grasshoppers*. Woodbridge: Blackbirch, 1998.

Perry, Phyllis Jean. *The Fiddlehoppers: Crickets, Katydids, and Locusts*. Danbury: Franklin Watts, 1995.

Ross, Michael Elsohn. *Cricketology*. Minneapolis: Carolrhoda, 1996.

Videos

Insect. Eyewitness Video Series.

Insects: Little Things that Run the World. NOVA Video Library.

Web Sites

http://www.ex.ac.uk/bugclub

The Bug Club Page has insect experts whom you can e-mail. The club organizes local field trips and publishes a newsletter.

http://www.le-foll.demon.co.uk/elen/toc.htm

The **Grasshoppers, Katydids, & Bush-crickets Page** has information on orthopterans, including fun facts, photos, and an insect game.

http://insects.ummz.lsa.umich.edu/yes/yes.html

The Young Entomologist's Society Page runs a program called "Bugs-on-Wheels." You may be able to arrange for an insect expert to visit your school and show your classmates some fascinating insects.

Index

About the Author

Sara Swan Miller has enjoyed working with children all her life, first as a Montessori nursery-school teacher and later as an outdoor environmental educator at the Mohonk Preserve in New Paltz, New York. As director of the preserve school program, Miller has led hundreds of school children on field trips and taught them the importance of appreciating and respecting the natural world, including its less lovable "creepy-crawlies."

Miller has written a number of children's books, including *Three Stories You Can Read to Your Dog*; *Three Stories You Can Read to Your Cat*; *Three More Stories You Can Read to Your Dog*; *What's in the Woods? An Outdoor Activity Book*; *Oh, Cats of Camp Rabbitbone*; *Piggy in the Parlor and Other Tales*; *Better Than TV*; and *Will You Sting Me? Will You Bite? The Truth About Some Scary-Looking Insects*. She has also written several books on farm animals for the Children's Press True Books series, a set of books on strange fishes, amphibians, reptiles, birds, and mammals for the Watts Library, and several other books in the Animals in Order series.